IMPERIA
VIENNA

I'm a Sunday's child, a child of the sun;
It entwined the golden rays into my throne
With its radiance it wove my crown
The sunlight is what I call my home
But if it ever left me I would die

Poem by Empress Elisabeth, 1887

The coordinates given in the text refer to the plan printed on the inside cover.

Opening times, entry prices etc. can be found on the related Internet homepage:

www.imperialvienna.info

verliebt
in Wien!

Holy water basin at the outer entrance to the catacombs

1010 Vienna,
Stephansplatz (I5)

St. Stephen's Cathedral in the heart of Vienna, with its towering spire, affectionately known to the Viennese as the "Steffl", is the very symbol of the city.

The cathedral did not, however, always mark the central point of Vienna.

In the 4th century AD what is now St. Stephen's Square lay just outside the walls of the Roman fortress of Vindobona. For centuries afterwards the area was a burial ground.

In 1732, when it had long since been incorporated into the city, Emperor Karl VI banned any further burials there, for hygienic reasons.

St. Stephen's is first mentioned in a document dated 1220 as a simple Romanesque parish church belonging to the bishopric of Passau.

In 1358 the Habsburg Duke Rudolf IV raised St. Stephen's to the status of an Austrian national shrine. One year later, he laid the foundation stone of a middle and late Gothic extension near the

present south tower.

The newly built nave, a three-aisle choir, originally enclosed the older building, but that was demolished in the early 15th century.

It took 74 years to build the almost 137-metre south tower, construction of which started in 1359 and was completed in 1433. It was the tallest building in Europe in its day. Rudolf IV is said to have laid the foundation stone with his own hands.

The dizzy height of the tower is not attributable to Rudolf, however, but to

ST. STEPHEN'S CATHEDRAL

The south side of the roof of the Albertine Choir with the Habsburg double-headed eagle and the year of the re-roofing, 1831.

1. The double cross supported by a double eagle was erected on the summit of the south tower during the reign of Emperor Leopold I. Previously, the emblem had been a six-pointed star combined with crescent of the new moon. This was, however, removed in 1686 after the 1683 Turkish siege had been defeated.

2. The Franciscan monk Johannes of Capistrano preached against the Turkish enemy from the Capistran Pulpit. The figure of the saint is enthroned over a Turkish soldier killed in battle.

3. The five-stage architecture of the main door to the cathedral.

the large number of architects and master masons who worked on it over the years and continually changed the building plans. His original concept of two towers of equal height was gradually abandoned, and only taken up again by Emperor Friedrich III in 1467. However, the difficulty of matching the formidable height of the south tower, and shortage of finance, led to the abandonment of the north tower project in 1511.

The uncompleted north tower now houses the carillon, including the Pummerin, the great bell of the cathedral.

The Romanesque Hei-
dentürme (Heathens'
Towers) are amongst the
cathedral's oldest building
elements. According to
legend the name Heiden-
türme originated in the
rule that unbaptised Chris-
tians were not allowed
to enter the body of the
church, but had to wait in
the anteroom beneath the
two towers.

THE INNER CITY

Wall painting at Kärntnerstrasse No. 16 (I6)

The inner city of Vienna is one of the most significant and impressive city centres in Europe.

The old city, extending over the entire First District, consists of broad, grandiose shopping streets like the Kärntnerstrasse (I6 -I7), the Graben (H5) and the Kohlmarkt (G5); flanked by baroque and classicist architectural masterpieces that set the viewer back into the time of the emperors.

Away from the bustling main streets there is a network of narrow, rambling streets and lanes of a romantic and even mystical character. In the Schönlaterngasse (K4) there is a house with an artistically painted facade, which tells the story of the basilisk, a legendary creature that is said to have cast its evil spells here.

1. The Kohlmarkt leading to St. Michael's Gate. The name Kohlmarkt originated in a period when coal and ashes could be obtained here. (G5)

2. The Griechengasse, the Greek Street (K4)

3. The Anker Clock (J4)

4. The square Am Hof (G4)

5. The Kaisergruft Habsburg mausoleum (H6)

6. The Judengasse, the Jewish Street (J4)

7. A view of St. Michael's Church (G5)

8. The Marriage Fountain, also known as the Joseph's Fountain, on the Hohen Markt square (I4)

9. Lobmeyr, purveyor of glassware to the imperial court, Kärntnerstrasse 26 (I6)

"Der liebe Augustin" was a Viennese character who entertained the people during the 1679 plague epidemic. One night, when he had drunk too much, he was found sleeping on the street. He was picked up for dead and was thrown into a mass grave outside the city walls along with other plague victims. When he awaked, he played his bagpipe until he was hauled out of the grave. To this day, "der liebe Augustin" is a symbol of the Viennese character and imperturbability. (K4)

The Basilisk House in the Schönlaterngasse (K4)

Christmas decorations on the Graben (H5)

Vienna's history goes right back to Roman times. The Roman legionary fortress of Vindobona, founded in the first century BC, had a marked influence on the future development of the city. Its traces can still be seen on the Michaelerplatz, where some of its wall foundations have been excavated and left exposed (see pp. 28-29).

In the Griechengasse is found the Griechenbeisel, reputably Vienna's oldest hostelry.

Furthermore, a large part of the street layout in the city goes back to Roman times. For example, the Graben (meaning "ditch"), now one of the most prestigious shopping streets in the city, gets its name from its position on the site of the former ditch that defended the Roman citadel.

The construction of multi-level underground cellars began under Habsburg rule. These were used as stores, workshops, and even as dwellings. Eventually, a huge network of tunnels connected all the cellars in the city. These cellars saved many lives during the bombing raids

of the Second World War.

There was also tragedy. The single entrance and stairs down to the official air raid shelter under the large Philipphof building complex was blocked by a direct bomb hit, so that several hundred people were buried alive and perished.

THE PLAGUE MONUMENT

1010 Vienna,
Graben (H5)

On the occasion of the major epidemic of bubonic plague that broke out in Vienna in 1679 Emperor Leopold I made a solemn promise to erect a monument (Pestsäule) as a reminder of the sufferings of the people. Johann Frühwirth completed the first wooden model that same year. It had nine angels around the base, and was crowned by the Holy Trinity.

Matthias Rauchmiller started to build the stone column from 1682 till 1686. After his sudden death, however, Johann Bernhard Fischer von Erlach comprehensively altered the plans, and the Pestsäule was finally finished in 1694 with the cooperation of numerous artists and craftsmen.

Over the richly ornamented pedestal can be seen the figure of an ugly old woman falling into the abyss. This symbolises the plague that has been overcome, but also metaphorically Christianity's victory over Islam – an expression of the trauma that Vienna had experienced during the Turkish sieges, most recently in1683. The female figure on the left, however, pointing a crucifix towards Heaven, symbolises the victory of the Catholic religion.

Above this, the kneeling Emperor Leopold I gazes up at the nine choirs of angels in the clouds above him, and at the golden Holy Trinity group that crowns the monument. The 18 metres high column, an outstanding example of the high baroque period in art, is Vienna's largest public monument, and stands as a symbol of Habsburg rule that was founded in faith.

VIENNA'S CHURCHES

Vienna's oldest church, the Ruprechtskirche St. Ruprecht's), reputedly founded around 740 AD, is first mentioned in writing in 1280 as the parish church of the city.

However, the legends surrounding many others, for example the Peterskirche (St. Peter's), also go back to the 8th century. The Emperor Charle-magne (Karl der Grosse) himself reputedly founded it in the year 792.

The Peterskirche now radiates the magnificence of its high baroque redesign, a masterpiece by Gabriel Montani and Lukas von Hildebrandt, with its impressive ceiling fresco by Johann Michael Rottmayr.

The Scottish Monastery (Schottenstift) on the Freyung square is Vienna's oldest of its kind. When it was founded in the 12th century it lay outside the city; the expansion of the town in the early 13th century finally brought it within the city walls.

The Gothic church of St. Maria am Gestade is so called because, before the regulation of the Danube in the 19th century, it stood on one of its steep banks (Gestade), but within the mediaeval city walls. It was first mentioned in the records in 1137.

The Church of the Franciscan Friars (Franziskanerkirche) is one of Austria's best-preserved examples of a late Renaissance sacred building.

A much younger masterpiece of high baroque architecture was planned by Johann Bernhard Fischer von Erlach: the Karlskirche (Church of St. Charles Borromeo), the roof of which offers a wonderful view over the city. It was founded by Emperor Karl VI in 1713, the year of the last great plague epidemic. The life of St. Charles Borromeo is depicted on the two impressive pillars that flank the main entrance.

Right up to the 17th

1.   St. Ruprecht's Church (J3-4)

2.   St. Charles Borromeo (H-I9)

14

century, the dual pillars of the Habsburg monarchy, the Church and the State, were indissolubly bound up with one another. The priesthood lost some of its power for the first time in the 18th century under Archduchess and Empress Maria Theresia, who removed the school system Catholic Church could take place under Emperor Franz Joseph, and the Josephine system finally ended with the suppression of the 1848 revolution.

The Church of St. Francis of Assisi was built in 1898 to commemorate the 50th anniversary of

from Church control and placed it under civil administration.

Her son, Emperor Joseph II, eliminated most of the clerical influence and forbade further contact between the Austrian Church and the Vatican. It took two generations before a restoration of the Franz Joseph's accession to the thrones of the Danube Monarchy. It was also the year of the tragic death of Empress Elisabeth.

Antonio Canova's famous tomb for Marie Christine, one of Empress Maria Theresia's daughters, is in St. Augustine's Church (H6). The entrance to the tomb is flanked by female figures representing the various ages of women. The tomb itself is empty, because, like all the other Habsburgs, Marie Christine was buried in the Monastery of the Capuchin Friars.

THE BURGGARTEN

Emperor Franz Joseph I (G7)

1010 Vienna,
Burggarten (G7)

The Burggarten, Emperor Franz Joseph's private garden, is probably the oldest park on the Ringstrasse. The site was a mediaeval paradise garden first mentioned in the year 1339. The idyllic garden is famous not only for the statue of Wolfgang Amadeus Mozart (see also "Vienna and Music", p. 74), but also for its palm house, built by Friedrich Ohmann 1902 to 1906 in secessionist Jugendstil. The park was opened to the public after the First World War and is now a popular venue on warm summer days.

THE HOFBURG

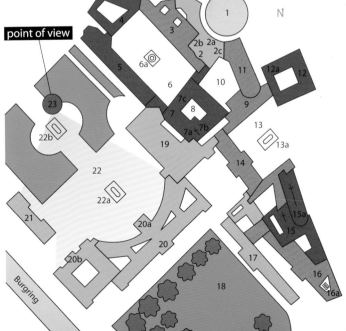

point of view

N

The Swiss Gate gives access to the Swiss Court, named after the Swiss Guard that at one time provided security for the Hofburg. The rollers for the drawbridge chains over the arch are a reminder of the days when access to the citadel was over the moat here.

1010 Vienna,
Hofburg (G6)

The Hofburg palace complex, with a total area of 240,000 m², 18 wings and 19 courtyards, is the largest palace complex in Europe. It is not only the official seat of the Austrian Federal President, but also serves numerous international organisations as a congress centre. It houses a number of museum exhibitions like the world's largest collection of historic music instruments, the world's largest papyrus collection, the Empress Elisabeth Museum, the Ephesos Museum, and the Court Hunting and Armour Museum.

The old castle was mentioned for the first time in the records in 1275, when it is assumed that Ottokar II Přemysl, King of Bohemia, Duke of Austria, Carinthia and Carniola, completed the building of the four-square Gothic citadel with its four towers that had been begun by the Babenberg dynasty he defeated in the 13th century.

Then, on 12 August 1278, Rudolf I von Habsburg defeated Ottokar in a battle on the Marchfeld, to the north-east of Vienna. For the next seven centuries, until 1918, the Habsburg dynasty expanded their power with the Hofburg as the centre of their might.

In the course of time the Hofburg developed into a complex of individual wings and small four-square citadels with an intricate network of secret passages and stairways. Whenever a Habsburg ruler ascended the throne he would have his predecessor's secret passages blocked up and his own built. To date, around 30 of these secret routes have been discovered in the course of the constant maintenance and building works.

THE OLD HOFBURG

This was how, in the confusion of the First World War in 1917, Emperor Karl I was able to carry on secret armistice negotiations with the French, which unfortunately came to nothing. This episode has gone into the history books as the "Sixtus Affair".

Under Emperor Ferdinand I from 1534 to 1566 the old citadel was remodelled in Renaissance style. This, the oldest part of the entire complex, is now known as the Swiss Court Wing. It was in Ferdinand's reign that the large central square now called "In der Burg" was laid out as a tournament ground for the later Emperor Maximilian II. The famous Schweizertor (Swiss Gate), that connects the square "In der Burg" with the Schweizerhof (Swiss Court) was also built during that first phase, in 1552/53.

The Amalienburg wing, completed in 1611, received its name from Empress Amalie Wilhelmine von Braunschweig, consort of Emperor Joseph I, who settled here after the death of her husband.

The Vienna Boys' Choir sings for Mass every Sunday in the Hofburg Chapel

During the 19th century these rooms were the residence of Empress Elisabeth.

Since the 17th century the entire gigantic complex has been known as the Hofburg. Emperor Leopold I inaugurated the work to connect all its various wings to give it its present character as a single fortress. The Leopoldine wing was the first secular baroque building in Vienna. It contains the most magnificent of all the Habsburg apartments, and is presently the seat of the President of the Republic of Austria.

Finally, Johann Bernhard Fischer von Erlach inaugurated the transition to the high baroque style with the building of the former Court Library, now the National Library of Austria, for Emperor Karl VI in 1722-1726.

1. A reproduction of the crown of the Holy Roman Empire of the German Nation towers the balustrade of the Imperial Chancellery Wing.

2. The square In der Burg with the statue of Emperor Franz II/I

3. Sentry box in front of the Amalienburg Wing

4. The tower of the Amalienburg Wing has a late 17th century sundial, a clock dating from the mid-19th century, and a moving globe that shows the phases of the moon.

5. The historic Deutschmeister military band at one of its regular Saturday concerts in the Hofburg every summer.

6. The Imperial Chancellery Wing with the portal through to the St. Michael's Wing, flanked by two statues of Hercules. The left one shows him in battle with the giant Antaeus, and on the right he is being aggressive towards the Egyptian king Busiris. The numerous statues of Hercules in the Hofburg go back to Emperor Karl VI, who identified himself with the major heroes of Greek mythology.

THE TREASURY

Emperor Franz I of Austria wearing Emperor Rudolf's II Crown

The Schatzkammer (Treasury, G6), dating back to the 14th century, contains secular and ecclesiastical chambers.

The Orb and Sceptre of the Austrian Empire were added by Emperor Matthias

Two showpieces stand out among the many treasures held in the secular chamber.

One of them is the crown of the Holy Roman Empire of the German Nation. Emperor Karl der Grosse (Charles the Great or Charlemagne), founder of the Empire in the year 800, was often pictured incorrectly with the imperial crown in order to legitimise the Habsburg claim to the sovereignty of the Roman-German Empire. Albrecht Dürer's famous portrait, painted several centuries later, was as much propaganda as high art. Nowadays, however, it is believed that Karl der Grosse never actually had the crown in his hands, since it is of later date in the 10th century.

The second showpiece is the crown of the Austrian Empire, which Emperor Franz II/I declared to be its official insignia after the proclamation of the new Empire in 1804. Formerly the Habsburg family house crown, it was created in Prague in the early 17th century.

Another highlight of the collection is the tabard of the Herald of the Austrian Empire. Probably dating from the early 19th century, the

Karl der Grosse (Charlemagne) by Albrecht Dürer

front side of the magnificent garment is embroidered with the double-headed eagle of the Habsburg imperial arms. The crowns on its two heads

The Orb of the Holy Roman Empire of the German Nation

Emperor Rudolf II's Crown, since 1804 the official insignia of the Austrian Empire

The Crown of the Holy Roman Empire of the German Nation

represent the kingdoms of Hungary and Bohemia, with the Austrian imperial crown over both. On its breast the eagle carries the arms of the House of Habsburg, sur- rounded by the arms of the imperial crown lands.

Another collection is the artifacts of the Order of the Golden Fleece, the supreme Habsburg order of chivalry.

The ecclesiastical cham- ber of the Treasury was first opened to the public during the 18th century by order of Archduchess and Empress Maria Theresia.

The tabard of the Herald of the Austrian Empire

ST. MICHAEL'S GATE

1. An eagle enthroned on a golden globe, flanked by geniuses with laurel wreaths and trumpets

2. The Personification of Wisdom, flanked by the allegory of Justice on the right, and Power in the person of Hercules on the left (Sculptor: Johannes Benk)

3. The entrance to the Empress Elisabeth Museum, the Imperial Apartments, and the Imperial Silverware Collection

4. "Power on Land" by Edmund von Hellmer, 1897

5. "Power on the Sea" by Rudolph von Weyr, 1895

6. Detail of "Power on Land"

Emperor Karl VI was very keen to realise the plans of his predecessor Leopold I for unifying the Hofburg complex. The first draft plan (1724-1725) was by Johann Lukas von Hildebrandt. It foresaw the citadel being replaced by a new palace, with one facade extended towards the city wall.

Hildebrandt also proposed a semicircular space with a domed central tower on the city side, on the site of the present St. Michael's Gate (Michaelertor).

Some initial steps were taken towards realising these plans, with the building of the Chancellery wing, the Reichskanzleitrakt. It was used as the Chancellery of the Holy Roman Empire until 1806, and later as the residence of Emperor Franz Joseph I.

After the completion of the Chancellery wing, Joseph Emanuel Fischer von Erlach took over the direction of the building work. He designed and built a triumphal entry into the Hofburg in high baroque style.

Ferdinand Kirschner finally completed the present St. Michael's wing in 1889-1893 in late historicist style.

THE SPANISH RIDING SCHOOL

The history of the Spanish Court Riding School (Spanische Hofreitschule, G6) goes back to the 16th century.

In the beginning the riding school was no more than a "Ross-Tumbl Platz", an unroofed piece of ground outside the city wall that could not be used in bad weather.

The history of the Spanish Riding School as an institution goes back to at least 1572, when it was first mentioned in the records.

In 1729 Emperor Karl VI finally brought it into the Hofburg, where it has remained ever since.

The Spanish Riding School is very selective in the choice of its horses. The Lipizzaner stallions are bred ex-

clusively at the Piber stud in western Styria. It is here that the initially black or brown foals spend their younger years. When they are 7 to 10 years old they attain the pure white colouring of the mature stallions. Their training starts at around four years old and lasts for several years.

The Spanish Riding School is the only one of its kind in the world that remains true to the classical riding tradition of the Renaissance. The difficult figures that the animals must master include the capriole (middle left), originally for use in battle, which involves springing and striking out with the hind legs while in mid-air.

THE JOSEFSPLATZ

The palace wings surrounding the Josefsplatz (G6) were combined during the reign of Archduchess and Empress Maria Theresia, and the Redoutensäle halls were added in 1744-1748. These were burned out in a conflagration in 1992, but were restored and reopened for functions in 1997.

The statue of Emperor Josef II in the middle of the square was erected during the reign of Franz II/I. The depiction of Josef as a Roman conqueror, complete with toga and laurel wreath, expresses the Habsburg belief that they were the descendants of the ancient Roman emperors.

The Josefsplatz is also the address of the world-famous grand hall of the National Library.

Something that be-

The inscription on the Burgtor reads "Justitia regnorum fundamentum" (Justice is the foundation of kingdoms) – a favourite saying of Emperor Franz I of Austria, 1768-1835 (E6)

The Ceremonial Hall and the Theseus Temple in the Volksgarten (People's Garden) were built in the early 19th century under Franz II/I, who also had the outer gateway (Burgtor) erected on the 10th anniversary of the battle of Leipzig and the victory over Napoleon.

The architect Gottfried Semper extended the Hofburg still further in the mid-19th century.

In 1869 the city's fortified defensive walls were demolished, which left the outer open area free for development as a monumental imperial forum that would be unique in the world.

The plan was to construct two identical wings of the New Hofburg in strict historicist style, as well as two identical museums, of fine arts and natural sciences, on the other side of the Ringstrasse: the Kunsthistorisches Museum and the Naturhistorisches Museum. (See p. 48)

The New Hofburg (F6) was built in neobaroque style with Renaissance elements. Semper left Vienna while work was still in progress, and Carl von Hasenauer took over from him. Hasenauer, however, died suddenly, and Friedrich Ohmann, a pupil of Ferstel, continued the work in 1899.

1. The centrepiece of Viktor Tilgner's fountain is the Greek god of the sea Triton, carrying a nymph on his shoulder.

2. The Volksgarten, with the Burgtheater, Votivkirche and University in the background.

3. The Empress Elisabeth Memorial by Hans Bitterlich was created in 1907 from marble quarried at Laas in South Tyrol. Emperor Franz Joseph himself chose the location for the monument, and a large proportion of the Viennese population gave contributions towards the cost of the project.

THE RINGSTRASSE

The Ringstrasse, seen from the Epstein Palace with a view towards the Parliament, Rathaus and Burgtheater (E4-5)

When, in 1809, Napoleon's French army blew up the Hofburg bastion, it was made clear to the Viennese that their city walls offered no defence against modern weaponry.

The old fortifications were retained for a long time, however, because of fears of a revolution. And even after the 1848 revolution numerous plans for expansion failed because of military opposition.

Nevertheless, on 20 December 1857, Emperor Franz Joseph I issued the order to demolish the defensive city wall. Instead, there would be a parade boulevard, the military character of which would be underlined by a defensive triangle of three barracks.

Even the 57 metres width of the Ring Road was based on military strategy.

An architectural competition brought prize-winning designs from Ludwig Förster, Friedrich Stache, Eduard van der Null and August Sicard von Sicardsburg. These formed the basis for the ground plan the Emperor finally approved in 1859 for the layout of the Ringstrasse, although this was frequently altered during the construction.

The Ringstrasse as a whole is regarded as a

work of Viennese historicism. The three decades it took to complete it have gone into the history books as "the Ringstrasse era".

The prestigious boulevard forms a ring around the old city of Vienna, and connects it with the inner suburbs that were incorporated into the city in 1850.

In the first phase, after the completion of the Court Opera House (now the Vienna State Opera), it was the prestigious town houses of the upper middle classes that imprinted the character of the Ring.

The imperial forum consisting of the Hofburg and the museums of Fine Arts and Natural History was to be an imposing testimony to the might of the Austrian Monarchy, but it was never fully completed.

The military character of the Ringstrasse was eventually mitigated by the completion of the civic forum comprising the Parliament, Rathaus (City Hall) and University.

Although ceremonially opened on 1 May 1865, the Ringstrasse was completed just before the First World War, after the Emperor had approved the demolition of the Franz Joseph Barracks and the development of the Stuben district.

THE VIENNA STATE OPERA

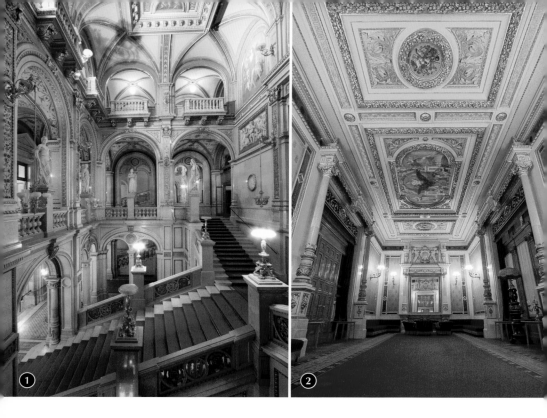

1010 Vienna,
Opernring 2 (H7)

The architects August Sicard von Sicardsburg and Eduard van der Nüll were delighted when, in 1861, they won the commission to design the new Vienna Court Opera House.

They decided to build it in Italian Renaissance style in commemoration of Eleonora Gonzaga, wife of Emperor Ferdinand II, who had brought opera from Italy to Vienna.

This first monumental building on the new Ringstrasse was intended to become the highlight of the Viennese romantic historicist movement and raise the city to new heights of prestige.

But the elation of the architects was premature.

The building work dragged on for over eight years in a period when the architectural taste of the Viennese public changed strongly, with the result that the Opera House was seen as outdated, even before its completion.

Meantime, the level of the Ringstrasse was raised by one metre, so that only three steps remained of the imposing entrance stairs that the Viennese regarded as so important for a representative building. The joke went around that it had "sunk".

When the Emperor

There are guided tours of the State Opera outside performance times.

1. The early historicist staircase of the State Opera

2. The Tea Salon (formerly the Emperor's Room) was destroyed in 1945, but was rebuilt by Otto Prossinger and Felix Cevela. The ceiling and walls are decorated with 22-carat gold leaf.

3. Eight sculptures by Hans Grasser decorate the fountains at the side wings of the building. The allegories, of Music over Frivolity, Joy and Solemnity (this photo), and the Lorelei over Grief, Love and Vengeance, reflect the different themes of opera.

4. The auditorium with the former imperial box (now the presidential box).

himself expressed criticism of the building it was too much for van der Müll. The architect committed suicide on 4 April 1868.

Sicard von Sicardsburg did not survive the completion of the Opera House either. He fell victim to a stroke on 11 June 1868.

The Court Opera House was completed by Gustav Gugitz and Joseph Storck, and was ceremonially opened on 25 May 1869 with a performance of Mozart's "Don Giovanni".

Nowadays the Vienna State Opera, its stage equal in size to its auditorium, makes an enormous contribution to Vienna's musical and other cultural prestige. Its international fame is due in no small measure to television transmissions of the Opera Ball, and its close association with the Vienna Philharmonic Orchestra.

The Habsburgs amassed formidable collections of artistic and scientific treasures over the centuries. Emperor Franz I Stephan, husband of Archduchess Maria Theresia, sponsored numerous expeditions to foreign countries in order to expand these collections.

The imperial family's treasures were scattered over a multitude of residences for lack of a central repository. Then, in the 19th century, Emperor Franz Joseph I commissioned Gottfried Semper to develop the idea of an imperial forum. This was to consist of two palace-like museums – the present museums of Fine Arts and of Natural History – as well as a new Hofburg complex on the other side of the Ringstrasse (see p. 20).

(see p. 20)

Semper died in Rome in 1879, and Carl von Hasenauer took over direction of the project.

The identical museums face each other from opposite sides of the Maria-Theresien-Platz.

The first to be completed, the Museum of Natural History, was formally opened on 10 August 1889. Its oldest exhibits go back to Emperor Franz I Stephan, who accumulated the then most important collection of specimens around 1750.

Its youngest exhibits are probably the bees that live in one of the exhibition rooms – separated from the visitors by glass!

It took 20 years to build the Museum of Fine Arts, from 1871 to its formal opening on 17 October 1891. Construction took nine years, and the internal architecture another eleven, with contributions by

noted artists like the Klimt brothers Gustav and Ernst.

Its collection of paintings reflects the countries that were formerly under Habsburg rule – and patronage. It is particularly famous for works by Pieter Bruegel the Elder as well as Albrecht Dürer, Rembrandt and Raffael.

Both museums not only look like palaces from the outside. Their interior decoration is marked by a love of detail, and is even more impressive than the outer facades. (Interior views of the Museum of Fine Arts)

1

3

2

1. The imperial forum was never completed, but remains the crowning point of the Ringstrasse project. The Museum of Fine Arts (right) and the Natural History Museum (left) were designed by Gottfried Semper.

2. Adam and Eve, by Bartholomaeus Spranger, 1593. (Museum of Fine Arts)

3. The Egyptian collection of the Natural History Museum.

4. The dinosaur collection of the Natural History Museum.

1. The statue of Archduchess and Empress Maria Theresia is the largest individual monument around the Ringstrasse. The pedestal is surrounded by figures of famous contemporary generals and artists, including the young Wolfgang Amadeus Mozart.

2. Christmas time always gives Vienna a festive atmosphere. Thousands of visitors come every year to experience the atmosphere of the traditional Christkindlmärkte.

3. A tour of inner Vienna by Fiaker (the name refers to both the coach and the coachman) can be had in any weather. The historic coaches are one of the sights of the city.

THE PARLIAMENT

1010 Vienna,
Dr.-Karl-Renner-Ring 3 (C-E5)

In Hungary and elsewhere in the Monarchy there was rising pressure for national autonomy. And so, in 1861, Emperor Franz Joseph made a serious attempt to unite his empire under his own rule. The Imperial Constitution of 1861 set up a new two-chamber Parliament (Reichsrat) with upper and lower Houses.

Since, however, the new Constitution had been drafted without the participation of the existing Parliament, the Monarchy was still far from a comprehensive constitutional system.

The members of the Herrenhaus (Upper House), with no higher limit to their numbers, were personally selected by the Emperor, whereas the

1. The flags fly only when the Parliament is in session.

2. The goddess Pallas Athene's helmet is adorned with an Egyptian sphinx and winged horses. (Sculptor: Alois Düll)

3. Nike, the Greek goddess of victory, with a laurel wreath in her hand (Sculptor: Alois Düll)

343 members of the Abgeordnetenhaus (Lower House) were elected by the provincial assemblies.

Legislation required not only adoption by both Houses, but also approval by the Emperor, a procedure that enable the ruler to block new laws.

The two Houses of the Reichsrat were originally accommodated in separate buildings: the Herrenhaus in what is

1. The base of the Pallas Athene statue is surrounded by the allegories of four major rivers: Danube and Inn (photo) by H. Haerdtl, and Moldau (Vltava) and Elbe by C. Kundmann.

2. The imposing pillared main entrance hall of the Parliament.

3. A quadriga group on the roof, driven by the winged Nike.

4. The original main chamber, now used for joint sessions of both houses of Parliament.

now the Justice Palace, and the Abgeordneten-haus in the present Academy of Fine Arts.

In October 1864 an architectural competition was announced for the erection of a building to house the new combined Reichsrat on the former military parade ground. The winner was the Danish architect Theophil von Hansen, who, with the Parliament, created one of the most important of the monumental buildings along the Ringstrasse.

With its allusions to the classical architecture of ancient Greece, which fascinated Hansen, the majestic Imperial Parliament building now houses the legislature of the Republic of Austria.

During the Monarchy the two Houses of the Reichsrat had their chambers in each of the side wings of the building.

The north side of the Parliament is decorated with statues of famous Austrian intellectuals, as a reminder of the constitutional monarchy of ancient Rome under Emperor Augustus, who did not enjoy unrestricted power as a monarch.

This wing contains the former chamber of the Abgeordnetenhaus, a multinational parliament with 33 parties from 8 nations and a total of 11 languages. Of these, German was declared the official parliamentary language, a circumstance that appreciably hindered communication. The historic chamber, which has been preserved in its original condition, is now used for sessions of the Bundesversammlung, a meeting of both Houses of the present republican Parliament.

The south wing of the building, which contains

Four quadriga groups on the roof, driven by winged Nikes, mark the outlines of both "High Houses".

the chamber of the former Herrenhaus, is adorned with statues of Greek philosophers, in recognition of their significance for the development of democratic principles.

The chamber was totally destroyed in the Second World War, but was rebuilt in a modern style by M. Fellerer and E. Wörle in the early 1950s. Since 1956 it has been the meeting place of the Nationalrat, the first House of the modern Austrian Parliament. The Bundesrat, the second House of the modern Parliament, meets in a smaller hall in the same wing that was formerly an antechamber and concourse for the Herrenhaus of imperial days.

Both Houses of the Imperial Reichsrat were joined by a dominating central wing modelled on the famous Temple of Erechtheios on the Acropolis in Athens, which is also the main entrance and core of the building. It was here, in the central pillared hall, 40 metres long and 23 metres wide, that sessions of the Imperial Parliament were to be opened by a speech from the throne by the Emperor in person.

In fact, Emperor Franz Joseph I never set foot in the new seat of the Reichsrat, and continued to hold his throne speech in the Hofburg on the other side of the Ringstrasse.

THE RATHAUS

1010 Vienna,
Rathausplatz 1 (C4)

Vienna is the capital of Austria, but it is also one of the nine federal provinces (Länder) in its own right. For this reason, the council chamber in the Rathaus (City Hall) is the seat, not only of the Vienna city administration, but also of the Landtag (Vienna Provincial Government).

The Gothic revival building is regarded as the principal example of late Viennese strict historicism.

The typically Gothic vertical design is repeatedly interrupted by horizontal Renaissance elements, for example the sills, which raises strong associations with French religious buildings.

The Rathaus has one of the largest interior courtyards in Europe. 331 steps lead up to the top of the dominant central tower.

Emperor Franz Joseph I laid down a condition to the architect, Friedrich von Schmidt, that the Rathaus tower was not to be higher than the 99 metre high twin spires of the nearby Votive Church. Schmidt managed to get round this, however. The tower is only 97.9 metres high, but the crowning 5.4 metres high figure of the knight (Rathausmann) holding the flagpole on its summit gives the tower a total height of 103.3 metres.

The Rathausmann is the very symbol of the City of Vienna. The figure, which weighs 650 kilograms, can stand up to any weather thanks to a spherical counterweight weighing 800 kilograms.

Since 1985 it has been possible to admire a copy of the Rathausmann in the park in front of the building.

The City Hall is also surrounded by legends, one of which is particularly often related:

In 1882 Friedrich von Schmidt celebrated the completion of the tower on the scaffolding at its summit by drinking three glasses of wine – with toasts to the Emperor, to the fatherland, and to the Viennese people.

When he threw the glasses from the tower to the ground, the first two shattered, but the third remained by a miracle intact.

1. The "Rathausmann" on the top of the tower of the City Hall.

2. Throughout the year there are many attractive events on the Rathausplatz in front of the City Hall. These range from the summer film festival from July to September, and the "Christkindl-markt" at Christmas. One special attraction is the Vienna "Ice Dream" (Eistraum), when the square becomes a skating rink.

3. The Rathausturm

THE BURGTHEATER

1010 Vienna,
Dr.-Karl-Lueger-Ring 2 (E3-4)

For the first time in the history of the Ringstrasse project the architects of the Imperial and Royal Court Theatre were not chosen by competition, but were appointed by the Emperor personally. The commission went in 1871 to Gottfried Semper and Carl von Hasenauer, the architects of the Imperial Forum (see The Museums of Fine Arts and Natural History, page 48, and The Hofburg, page 20). One of the reasons was that Semper had had concrete plans for linking the theatre with the projected west wing of the New Hofburg by a bridge or similar construction.

In 1876 Semper had to move to Rome for health reasons, and the west wing of the Hofburg was never built.

Hasenauer took over the sole responsibility for the project, and in 1888 the Hofburgtheater was completed as a freestanding building complex.

The monumental late historicist building, strongly orientated towards the Italian Renaissance with a number of baroque elements, was ceremonially inaugurated that same year with Grillparzer's "Esther" and Schiller's "Wallenstein".

The new Court Theatre was initially anything but popular with the public on

account of its poor acoustics and sight.

However, these drawbacks could be corrected in 1897 by a reconstruction of the auditorium.

In 1945 the Burgtheater (as it was renamed by the Republic) was severely damaged by aerial bombing.

Ten years later, it reopened on 15 October 1955 with a performance of Franz Grillparzer's "König Ottokars Glück und Ende".

Its outer facade is another architectural masterpiece with considerable attention to detail.

The windows of the first floor are surmounted by the names of great literary figures like Schiller, Grillparzer, Goethe and Shakespeare, with character heads by the sculptor Viktor Tilgner.

The windows are flanked by role figures from the famous works by the poets, sculpted by Rudolph von Weyr.

The Greek god Apollo, by Carl Kundmann, is enthroned above the balustrade of the Burgtheater.

THE UNIVERSITY

Three of the four corner paintings on the ceiling of the University's festival hall were to have been painted by Gustav Klimt. This, however, caused a scandal, in view of Klimt's break with the then accepted norms, so that he withdrew from the commission. Since 2005 reproductions of the Klimt paintings, which were burned in 1945, have been mounted on the ceiling.

1010 Vienna,
Dr.-Karl-Lueger-Ring 1 (E3)

The Alma Mater Rudolphina Vindobonensis was founded in 1365 by Duke Rudolph IV, known as Rudolph the Founder, and is thus the oldest university in the German-speaking region.

The old University of Vienna, not far from St. Stephen's Cathedral, was one of the hotbeds of the 1848 revolution. After it had been suppressed, the young Emperor Franz Joseph planned to relocate the individual faculties among the suburbs of the city, in order to hinder further student uprisings.

However, thanks to the efforts of Vienna's mayor, Cajetan Felder, the architect Heinrich Ferstel finally received the commission to erect a central university building on the Ringstrasse. The imperial monumental building was ceremonially opened in 1884.

At the end of The Second World War it was the target of 26 bomb hits. Despite the resulting damage and the necessary reconstruction work, the first lectures started again at the end of May 1945.

Today, the University of Vienna, with 15 faculties, numerous institutes and around 85,000 students, extends over more than 60 locations in the city.

THE VOTIVE CHURCH

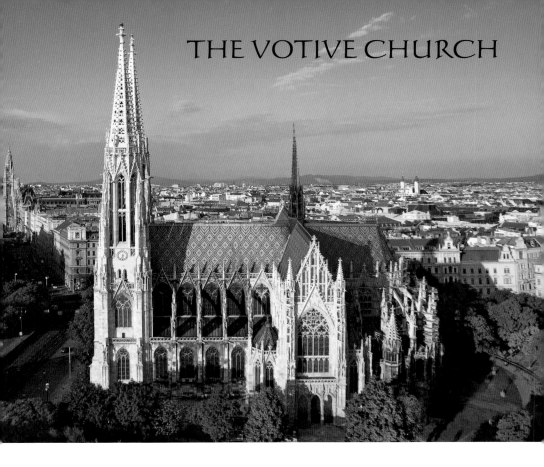

1090 Vienna,
Rooseveltplatz (C1)

The Votivkirche is one of the sights of Vienna. Its fame is due largely to the history of its foundation.

On 18 February 1853 the 23-year-old Emperor Franz Joseph was strolling along the defensive bastion of the inner city when the Hungarian tailor János Libenyi attacked him with a knife.

It is said that the Em-peror's stiff uniform collar saved him from serious injury, so that he got off with a small wound on his throat. The would-be as-sassin was later executed for attempted murder.

The Emperor's brother, Archduke Ferdinand Maxi-milian, inaugurated a cam-paign to build a church as thanks to God for saving the Emperor's life. Sub-scriptions were solicited from all over the Mon-archy. The architectural competition to build it was won by the already estab-lished Heinrich Ferstel.

The foundation stone of the "Ringstrasse Cathedral" was laid on 24 April 1856, the second anniversary of the wedding of Franz Joseph and Empress Elisa-beth.

The church was finally dedicated in 1879 on the silver wedding anniversary of Franz Joseph and Elisa-beth, after a building pe-riod of 23 years.

THE OLD STOCK EXCHANGE

1010 Vienna,
Schottenring 16 (G2)

The Vienna Stock Exchange was founded in 1771 under Archduchess and Empress Maria Theresia, and is thereby the oldest institution of its kind in the world.

The first stock exchange crash occurred in 1873, with disastrous worldwide effects that were also felt in Vienna.

The efforts by the stock exchange management to find a suitable location for its transactions led to the erection of the imposing building on the Schottenring in 1873-1877. The architect was Theophil Hansen.

He executed the commission as a four-square complex with the transaction hall in the centre. A fire destroyed the hall in 1956.

The basilica-like character of the two-storey hall was intended to symbolise the function of the stock exchange as a financial cathedral.

Since the rebuilding in 1959 the centre of the building complex has been a large and spacious interior courtyard.

The Vienna stock exchange attained considerable prominence due to the international political and economic standing of the Habsburg Monarchy as one of the five great powers of its day.

The stock exchange remained closed during the First World War.

When it reopened in 1919 it experienced a continuous upward swing. However, the world economic crisis in the 1930s left deep traces in Vienna, and the stock prices recovered only very slowly during the following years.

The modern, electronically operated Vienna Stock Exchange, the Wiener Börse AG, is located in the Caprara-Geymüller Palace in the Wallnerstrasse.

ARSENAL AND ROSSAU BARRACKS

The 1848 revolution had a massive effect on the strategic planning of Vienna. Emperor Franz Joseph I had three defensive army barracks built in the vicinity of three rail stations, in order to be able to bring troops into the city as swiftly as possible in the event of further insurrection.

The Franz Joseph Barracks, erected in 1852-1857, were demolished in 1901 in order to make way for the development of the present Stuben district around the south-east part of the Ringstrasse.

In the Third District, in the south of Vienna, from where Prince Alfred Windisch-Graetz with his artillery fought against the rebels in the city, the massive Arsenal was built in a romantic historicist style. When it was finished in 1857 it lay outside the defensive walls that still surrounded the city. Nowadays it houses the Museum of Military History (Heeresgeschichtliches Museum).

The Rossau Barracks building (below right) was built in 1865-1869. Its name stems from the Rossau (horse meadow) beside the arm of the river called the Danube Canal, where the cavalry horses were watered.

The building of these barracks caused massive resentment and criticism among the population on account of their purpose for the suppression of civil unrest.

THE STADTPARK

1010 Vienna,
Parkring (L7)

The Stadtpark (City Park), which lies directly on the Stubenring, is the oldest public park in Vienna, and the largest green space in the Inner City. Opened in 1857, it was converted into an English garden in 1860. It includes the famous Kursalon Wien, where Johann Strauss (son) played in person on many occasions. The numerous features of its Jugendstil layout include the famous golden statue of Johann Strauss and a memorial to Franz Schubert.

1. The view from the Hotel Intercontinental to the Stadtpark with its Jugendstil promenade by Friedrich Oh-mann and Joseph Hackhofer (1903-1906).

2. The duck pond in the Stadt-park, a coloured lithograph dated 1862.

VIENNA AND MUSIC

The Vienna Philharmonic at their annual Midsummer Night Concert in the park of Schönbrunn Palace. The open-air event, with free admission, attracts up to 120,000 music lovers.

No other town or city in the world shares that indelible association with classical music that is the hallmark of Vienna.

As late as the 18th century music was still largely the prerogative of aristocratic society.

However, during the Biedermeier period, up to the 1848 revolution, musical life gradually moved into the coffee houses and salons of the wider Viennese society.

During the second half of the 19th century, increasing demand by the emerging middle classes led to the building of the first concert halls.

The Society of Friends of Music (Gesellschaft der Musikfreunde), founded in 1812, still makes a major contribution to preserving and archiving the works of the principal composers.

It cooperates closely with the Vienna Philharmonic Orchestra in the Musik-verein building erected by Theophil Hansen in 1867 to 1870. The Philharmonic, founded by Otto Nicolai in 1842, gave its first concert in the large Redoutensaal of the Hofburg. To the present day, only musicians employed in the orchestra of the Vienna State Opera (the former Court Opera) can become members of the Vienna Philharmonic.

Richard Wagner described the Philharmonic as one of the world's most pre-eminent orchestras. His fellow-composer Richard Strauss remarked: "To praise the Philharmonic is to carry violins to Vienna".

1. *The Musikverein (Architect Theophil Hansen)*

2. *The Vienna Philharmonic's world-famous New Year Concert in the Golden Hall of the Musikverein. With its traditional emphasis on the music of the Strauss dynasty it is one of the world's major cultural events. Relayed to the television services of over 70 countries, it is enjoyed by around 50 million viewers all round the world.*

Even at an earlier date aristocratic patronage attracted the best musicians of their day to Vienna. Joseph Haydn (1732-1809), Wolfgang Amadeus Mozart (1756-1791) and Ludwig van Beethoven (1770-1827) were the foremost pioneers of the Viennese classical tradition.

The city itself also produced some outstanding native composers. Joseph Lanner (1801-1843) and Johann Strauss senior (1804-1849) left their imprint on the music that even today is most closely associated with the city: the world-famous Viennese waltz.

The "Radetzky March" by the elder Strauss was first heard in 1848, the "Year of Revolutions", and

1. The Mozart Memorial in the Burggarten, by E. Tilgner (F7)

2. Mozart's grave, St. Marx Cemetery

3. Mozart, played by a street artist

4. Haydn memorial in front of the Mariahilf Church, by H. Natter

is now one of the most famous marches of all time.

His son, also Johann Strauss (1825-1899), whose "Blue Danube" waltz rapidly became Vienna's unofficial anthem, was the great master of the operetta. His most famous one, "Die Fledermaus" (The Bat), received its first performance in the Theater an der Wien.

Numerous statues, fountains and memorials throughout Vienna commemorate the famous musicians who lived and worked here. Many of them have graves of honour in the Vienna Central Cemetery.

5. Beethoven memorial on the Beethovenplatz, by C. Zumbusch (K8)

6. Strauss-Lanner memorial on the Rathausplatz, by H. Seifert (C4)

7. Mozart Fountain in the Mozartgasse, by C. Wollek

8. Strauss memorial in the Stadtpark, by E. Hellmer (L7)

9.   Brahms grave in the Central Cemetery, by I. Conrat

10. Schubert memorial in the Stadtpark, by C. Kundmann (L7)

THE CONGRESS DANCES . . .

1

2

"Le congrès ne marche pas, il danse." (The Congress makes no progress, instead it dances.) This famous remark by the Belgian diplomat Charles Joseph de Ligne describes the situation at the court of Emperor Franz II/I in 1814/15 at the time of the Congress of Vienna that had been called to redraw the map of Europe after the end of the Napoleonic Wars. The Austrian Emperor, who was not normally noted for extravagance, spared no costs to entertain and impress his international elite guests with numerous balls and other prestigious events.

Even if the Congress did not bring the hoped-for success, and ended in a series of compromises, the House of Habsburg had succeeded in dem-

onstrating its majesty and wealth to the rest of Europe.

Even today, the Vienna ball season revolves around hundreds of events, with highlights like the Emperor Ball, the Philharmonic Ball, the Officers' Ball, the Flower Ball and the Opera Ball, a state occasion as well as a major social and cultural event.

1. The opening of the Officers' Ball in the Hofburg.

2. An officer of the Queen's Dragoon Guards from Wales at the Officers' Ball.

3. The Rudolfiner Redoute in the Hofburg. The features of a redoute are the ladies with masks, and the ladies' choice of partners.

4. The Flower Ball in the Rathaus.

5. The Philharmonic Ball in the Golden Hall of the Musikverein.

The Albertina is one of the best-known museums in Vienna.

The magnificent classicist palace was built in 1745-1757 beside the Hofburg for Count Emanuel Teles da Silva-Tarouca.

In 1763 it became the residence of Duke Albert von Sachsen-Teschen, who for the first time made his impressive collection of drawings and prints available for public viewing.

In 1918 the palace finally came into the possession of the Republic of Austria. The Albertina now houses the world's largest and most important collection of graphic art.

Another major private collection is that of the Liechtenstein aristocratic family that is housed in the Liechtenstein Palace Museum. It was regarded as one of the finest private collections in the world, even before its removal to safety out of Vienna during the Second World War.

The Museum of Applied Art, built by Heinrich Ferstel on the Ringstrasse, contains a permanent ex-

VIENNA'S MUSEUMS

hibition as well as a study collection and a gallery.

The Museums Quarter (MQ) Vienna that was opened in 2001 in the former imperial stables has long since become one of the most visited attractions in the city. It offers the culturally interested visitor a broad palette, including the Leopold Museum with the world's largest Egon Schiele collection and the Ludwig Trust's Museum of Modern Art.

The spacious inner courtyard of the former stablings has now become an attraction in its own right as a place for rest and recreation.

There seem to be no limits to the cultural diversity offered by Vienna's museums.

1. The Museum of Modern Art (C7)

2. Entrance to the Museums Quarter (C7)

3. A coach in the Liechtenstein Museum

4. Museum of Applied Art (M6)

5. The Albertina (G7)

SCHÖNBRUNN PALACE

1130 Vienna,
Schönbrunner Schloßstraße

The palace of Schönbrunn is one of the world's foremost cultural treasures. Its history goes back to the Middle Ages, when it lay far outside the walls of the city.

In the 14th century the Katterburg, as the area was known, with a dairy farm and a small mill on the River Vienna (Wienfluss), belonged to the Monastery of Klosterneuburg.

In the course of time it was taken over and extended by a number of

The Schönbrunn palace gardens are one of the seven most important Habsburg parks and gardens. Nowadays they are administered by the Federal Parks Service in Vienna and Innsbruck.

tenants, and eventually a grand mansion was built on the site.

During the 16th century Emperor Maximilian II took an interest in the property, especially on account of its outstanding hunting ground. He purchased the Katterburg in 1569, and erected an imperial hunting lodge with an attached menagerie for game animals.

When Maximilian died in 1576, his son Rudolph II succeeded him. He provided the finance to maintain the estate, but he never used it himself.

His brother Matthias, who ascended the

throne in 1612, revived hunting on the Katterburg. According to legend, it was he who discovered the natural spring that later gave its name to the estate: the Schöner Brunnen (beautiful fountain) that can still be admired in the palace park.

When Matthias died in 1619, his cousin Ferdinand II ascended the imperial throne.

The Emperor and his wife, Eleonora I von Gonzaga, often visited Schönbrunn for hunting, and when he died in 1637 Eleonora had a summer residence built there, and declared it to be her widow's seat.

Finished in 1642, this mansion was mentioned in the records for the first time under the name Schönbrunn.

This house was totally destroyed during the second siege of Vienna by the Turkish army in 1683.

In 1686 the estate came into the possession of Emperor Leopold I, who had a new representative residence built for his son Joseph I. Since money was no object for the Em-

1. The Nymph Fountain, with Schönbrunn Palace in the background

2. The view from the Gloriette hill down to the Palace

3. The Neptune Fountain, by J.F. Hetzendorf von Hohenberg

4. The labyrinth in Schönbrunn Park

5. The simulated Roman Ruin, by J.F. Hetzendorf von Hohenberg

peror when it came to catering for his son, he commissioned the famous architect Johann Bernhard Fischer von Erlach to draw up the plans. These entered the history books as the Schönbrunn I draft. They were, however, so expensive that not even the Emperor could afford to implement them.

It was the second draft that was finally realised in 1696 and gave the complex what is largely its present layout – partly on the foundations of the old mansion.

In 1728 Emperor Karl VI, brother of the deceased Joseph I, acquired Schönbrunn, which he had comprehensively redesigned.

It was under Archduchess and Empress Maria Theresia that Schönbrunn was to experience its first phase of splendour.

She developed it into an imperial residence for the first time in 1743-1763, and remodelled it in rococo style with rose-coloured facades and numerous ornaments.

Schönbrunn by now had more than 1,000 rooms, because apart from the imperial couple and their 16 children there were numerous court officials and servants who had to be provided with accommodation.

The six-year-old Wolfgang Amadeus Mozart played for Empress Maria Theresia in Schönbrunn Palace. At the end of his performance he is reported to have climbed onto her lap and kissed her.

Emperor Franz I Stephan von Lothringen, Maria Theresia's husband, took a great personal interest in the arts and natural sciences. He

The romantically situated Gloriette pavilion stands on the top of a hill overlooking Schönbrunn Palace. It was originally the idea that the Palace itself, designed to rival Versailles in Paris, should stand on the hill. The plan was abandoned when the hill was found to be too unstable to support the huge building.

expanded what is still the world's oldest zoo in the huge area of Schönbrunn Park.

The immediate reason for the expansion is reputed to have been the arrival at Schönbrunn in 1750 of a rhinoceros from India – at that time an extremely exotic introduction to Europe.

In 1753 Franz Stephan also opened the so-called Dutch Garden with plants from many foreign countries. The present monumental palm house was built on its site in

The Little Gloriette

1880-1882.

Maria Theresia took Franz Stephan's death in 1765 very hard. The widowed ruler spared no expense to furnish his memorial rooms in the east wing of the palace.

Johann Ferdinand von Hetzendorf was engaged to redesign the palace park that had been laid out by Jean Trehet in 1705. The Neptune Fountain, the Roman Ruin, the Obelisk and the Gloriette pavilion were all erected during the 1770s.

In 1779, one year be-

1. The memorial rooms in remembrance of Emperor Franz Stephan von Lothringen. The walls of the so-called "Vieux-Laque" room are decorated with colourfully painted Chinese enamel panels. These were painted on the high sea, in order to protect the wet enamel from dust.

2. The ceiling fresco in the Grand Gallery, by the Italian painter Gregorio Guglielmi, is one of the most impressive examples of its kind in Austria.

The Grand Gallery, 40 metres long and 10 metres broad, is one of the world's most significant rococo interiors.

fore Maria Theresia's death, Schönbrunn Park was opened to the public. Up to the beginning of the 19th century the palace itself remained largely unoccupied. Then Emperor Franz II/I started to use it again as a summer residence.

In 1805, and again in 1809, the French army occupied Vienna. Napoleon himself lived in Franz Stephan's memorial rooms in the palace.

In 1817-1819 Emperor Franz II/I had the facades redesigned by Johann Amann. Amann removed the rococo elements dating from the Maria Theresia period, and changed its colour to the present golden yellow.

Emperor Franz Joseph opened the Palm House in 1882

Emperor Franz Joseph I, who was born in Schönbrunn in 1830, inaugurated another golden age after he ascended the throne in 1848. Schönbrunn became his favourite residence in Vienna, and he spent the greater part of his time there when in the capital.

Towards the end of the Second World War the roof of the palace was hit by an unexploded bomb, which destroyed one of the three ceiling frescos in the Great Gallery, which show the allegories of the Austrian crown lands, Peace, and War. Ironically, it was the allegory of War that was destroyed.

It was only after the war that the ceiling could be repaired and the painting restored.

Even worse damage was caused to the famous Schönbrunn Zoo, with horrendous loss of life among the animals. The Soviet army commander, General Shepilov, saved the situation by diverting military rations to feed the starving animals.

In 1996 UNESCO listed the entire Schönbrunn ensemble with the imperial baroque palace, the extensive gardens, the oldest zoo in the world and the imposing glass palm house as objects of our cultural heritage.

1. Franz Stephan von Lothringen, the founder of Schönbrunn Zoo

2. Numerous wild creatures have also made their homes in the extensive grounds of Schönbrunn Park.

THE BELVEDERE

1030 Vienna,
Prinz Eugen-Straße 27

The Lower Belvedere

Around 1693 Prince Eugene of Savoy, Austria's greatest military leader, began to acquire areas of land along the Rennweg in what is now Vienna's Third District.

The first work to lay out these grounds as an extensive garden began in the early 18th century.

In 1714 Prince Eugene obtained permission from the Emperor to fence in his ground on the Rennweg.

This marked the official start of building work on the Lower Belvedere, which was completed two years later.

The project started to take shape under the direction of Johann Lukas von Hildebrandt, Eugene's favourite architect.

The building functioned initially as a residential palace, containing a marble banqueting hall, several luxurious residential

The special exhibitions in the Lower Belvedere are held in the "Orangerie", the former orange house of Prince Eugene's horticultural establishment.

rooms and a library, and at first housed the Prince's collection of art and antiques. After his death

in 1736, however, these were sold by his sole heiress, Duchess Viktoria von Sachsen-Hildburghausen.

The Belvedere came into possession of the imperial court in 1752, during the reign of Maria Theresia, but was never used by her.

The palace served temporarily as an imperial residence during the French Revolution.

During the Napoleonic wars the world-famous collections of Archduke Ferdinand II were brought here from Ambras Castle in Tyrol for a short period for safety.

After 1806 the Lower Belvedere also housed some of the imperial treasures. In 1891, however, these were removed to the newly opened Museum of Fine Arts on the Ringstrasse.

The building was again used as a residence until 1900, when it became a museum of contemporary art.

Since 1903 the Modern Gallery here has formed the basis for the modern collections.

The Upper Belvedere

The initial idea here was to erect a Gloriette pavilion, like that in Schönbrunn Park, in order to take advantage of the superb view over the city.

However, that soon gave way to Hildebrandt's plan to build another prestigious palace on Prince Eugene's ground.

The Upper Belvedere was constructed in the years 1717-1723. It is regarded to this day as the jewel of the ensemble.

Prince Eugene used it mainly for representative purposes.

After his death the Imperial Gallery of Paintings was installed here in 1781.

In 1891, however, this was transferred to the new Museum of Fine Art along with the collections in the Lower Belvedere.

A comprehensive programme of modernisation

in the Upper Belvedere began in 1897 under the architect E. von Förster.

Archduke Franz Ferdinand and his family took over the Belvedere in 1899. He had been heir to the thrones of Austria-Hungary since the tragic death of Crown Prince Rudolf in 1889.

With the assassination of Franz Ferdinand and his wife in Sarajevo on 28 June 1914, an event that sparked off the First World War, the function of the Belvedere as an imperial residence came to an end.

In 1919 the palace came into the possession of the young Republic of Austria and was adapted as a museum.

It was badly damaged during air raids in 1944-1945, and extensive renovation was necessary after the war.

The most important event during the post-war period was the formal signing of the Austrian State Treaty in May 1955. The ceremony was held in the Marble Hall of the Upper Belvedere.

As far as the Austrians were concerned, this was the event that got rid of the four armies that had occupied Austria for the previous ten years, and it re-established Austria as an independent nation within the world community.

The Austrian State Treaty was also a major turning point in the Cold War

between East and West, because it ushered in the era of peaceful coexistence that led on to the settlement of the major differences between the great powers.

The Belvedere Park

During the 1848 revolution the revolutionaries fighting the imperial troops used the park as a military camp.

A sphinx in the Belvedere Park

The then director, J. P. Krafft, led the comprehensive renovation that became necessary, with particular attention to preserving the valuable baroque building substance.

Krafft also inaugurated the present entrances to the palace and park.

The extensive ensemble, which at one time included an aviary and menagerie, is now one of the city's finest baroque parks.

THE HERMES VILLA

1130 Vienna,
Lainzer Tiergarten

The Hermes Villa in the Lainzer Tiergarten (Wild Life Park) lies in the city's 13th District, in a former imperial hunting park a little apart from the general bustle of the town. Emperor Franz Joseph had it built from 1882 to 1886 by Carl von Hasenauer, in a late romantic architectural style. He gave it as a present to his wife, Empress Elisabeth, in May 1884. The name is derived from the statue of the Greek god Hermes that stands in the gar-

The museum in the Hermes Villa has contained many exhibitions since 1978

den. Franz Joseph hoped that Elisabeth would find peace here from the eyes of the public and from the strict etiquette of the imperial court.

When she could finally occupy the house in1886, Elisabeth was not at first attracted to it. The not quite finished house lacked the atmosphere of a home, and the garden was still bare and incomplete.

She nevertheless found herself attracted to it, and even described it as her "Castle of Dreams".

Here she could also fol-

low her great passion of riding. Despite this, the wandering Empress did not spend much time in the Hermes Villa.

It was here that Franz Joseph wrote his last letter to Elisabeth – which, however, she never received.

On the following day, 10 September 1898, she was walking along the esplanade in Geneva when she was assaulted by a young Italian anarchist, who was actually out to assassinate a completely different royal personality.

He stabbed Elisabeth with a file. She did not realise the seriousness of the injury, and boarded a steamer, but then collapsed. She was taken back to her hotel in Geneva, but then died of her injuries a few hours later.

VIENNESE JUGENDSTIL

1. *Linke Wienzeile nos. 38 and 40, by architect Otto Wagner*

Otto Wagner, Gustav Klimt and many other revolutionary artists at the turn of the 20th century belonged to the group who broke away from the traditional art establishment to form the Vienna Secession.

In 1898 a new exhibition building was to be erected, and the choice of architect fell on the Hasenauer disciple Joseph Maria Olbrich.

The Secession, which is seen as a work of the art nouveau style, set the tone for the Viennese modern movement and is regarded as a precursor of Jugendstil.

The most striking feature of the building is its crown of gilded iron laurel leaves.

The most significant architectural figure of the Viennese Jugendstil movement is Otto Wagner, whose handwriting is seen on numerous buildings in the city. These include the two prominent residential blocks numbers 38 and 40 on the Linke Wienzeile. They have been much admired, but also criticised, on account of their modern flat facades, the one

The buildings and artworks depicted on these pages were all designed by Otto Wagner.

1. Otto Wagner Villa, later embellished by Ernst Fuchs (Hüttelbergstrasse 26)

2. The Steinhof Church (Baumgartner Höhe 1)

3. Former local rail station pavilion on the Karlsplatz (H9)

4. Details of the Steinhof Church

5. Detail of the imperial rail station pavilion (Schönbrunner Schloßstraße)

6. Detail of the Post Office Savings Bank on the Georg Coch Platz (L4)

THE VIENNESE CAFÉ

The Café Griensteidl around 1896   *The Café Hawelka*

The Kaffeehaus as the institution we know today became established in fin de siècle Vienna around 1900.

It was a time of contrasts between the mass of impoverished proletarian suburbs and the individualism of the wealthy upper middle class elite of the inner city.

At the end of the 19th century the atmosphere in the city was troubled, with numerous tumults and rebellious acts, as if the population sensed that the gradual decline of the Monarchy could no longer be prevented.

It was then that the Viennese Kaffeehaus crystallised into a meeting place for great minds like Sigmund Freud or Viktor Adler, who were concerning themselves with the human mind and with current social and political problems. Expressionists like Gustav Klimt and Egon Schiele established artistic values. Great Jugendstil architects like Otto Wagner had a significant influence on the city's built environment.

The Kaffeehaus was the focal point of that great Indian summer of Viennese culture that reached its high point around the year 1900, a phenomenon that remains to this day a subject of fascination and study around the world. It epitomises the final flowering of the Habsburg Monarchy, the echoes of which have by no means yet died away.

The most famous cafés included the Café Landtmann (E4), on the Dr. Karl Lueger Ring, that is still in family ownership; the literary Café Hawelka (H5) in the Dorotheergasse; and the Café Central (F4) in the Herrengasse, the regular meeting place for the writer Peter Altenberg, who even had his mail sent there.

The Café Sacher (H7), in the Hotel Sacher, is famous for its Sachertorte cake. The author Graham Greene was a regular guest here, where he wrote parts of his film script for "The Third Man".

The Café Central

THE VIENNESE KITCHEN

A genuine Viennese Schnitzel is best enjoyed at Figlmüller (J5)

The Habsburg Monarchy contained a large number of different nationalities, something that is reflected to this day in the vast range of culinary delights that can be sampled in Vienna. Many of the dishes originated in distant parts of the Monarchy. The classic Viennese Strudel, in its best-known variations made with apples or cottage cheese, probably came from Hungary. Powidltascherl (plum jam

in batter) and Buchteln (sweet yeast dumplings) came from Bohemia, and Vienna's Faschingskrapfen (filled doughnuts) probably originated in Venice. Emperor Franz Joseph's favourite dish was the fa-

mous Tafelspitz, a selected piece of beef served with chives sauce, roast potatoes and horseradish sauce. The Kaiserschmarren (chopped pancake with sugar and jam) and the popular Viennese Schnitzel (veal steak fried in butter with flour and egg) should also not be omitted from the long list of Viennese favourites that are enjoyed by the local gourmets as much as by their visitors.

THE NASCHMARKT

The Naschmarkt, in the vicinity of the Karlsplatz, is one of the most-frequented foodstuffs markets in Vienna.

Now more than 200 years old, it had its origins in a milk market on the Freyung square beside the Scottish Monastery. In earlier times it was known colloquially as an "Aschmarkt" – one theory being that the name was derived from the ash wood that was used to make the milk pails.

In the course of time the market was moved pro-gressively to the south un-til it found its present site

when the Wienfluss (River Vienna) was roofed over in the late 19th century. In 1916 Friedrich Jäckel built the present stands that give the market its character.

It is accepted that the name Naschmarkt (naschen = nibble) be-came current around 1820 on account of its wide range of culinary products from all over the world. To this day the market and the products it sells are a throwback to the days of the Monarchy. The stand personnel will-ingly allow customers to sample their wares.

THE PRATER

The Prater (Q1) is one of the major recreational features of Vienna. Its area of around 600 hectares includes the Volksprater with its green meadows and children's play areas, the Vienna Trade Fair exhibition centre, the Vienna Stadium, and the famous Wurstelprater with its fairground attractions.

The 4.5 km long Prater Hauptallee, from the Praterstern transport network to the Lusthaus restaurant, is a paradise for joggers and cyclists.

First mentioned in 1162, the Prater was in Habsburg ownership from the mid-16th century for hunting, and was opened to the public in 1766. Many aristocrats were enraged at having to share the place with the common herd. When Emperor Joseph II heard of this, he remarked that he would have to spend his

1. The Wurstelprater with the Riesenrad

2. Eating knuckle of pork in the famous Schweizerhaus

3. The Liliput Railway

4. The Achterbahn roller coaster

5. This nine-metre high figure is a reminder of the conjuror and roundabout owner Basilio Calafati, one of the early 19th-century proprietors in the Wurstelprater.

time in the Habsburg mausoleum in the Kaisergruft to be among his own people. Joseph was not egalitarian, but he pursued a policy of opening imperial property to the people.

Swings and roundabouts swiftly followed the opening of the first restaurants. The Calafati statue is a present reminder of a conjurer who opened a roundabout here.

The giant Ferris wheel, the Riesenrad, was erected in 1897 as an advance contribution to Emperor Franz Joseph's fiftieth anniversary celebrations, and has since been one of the major symbols of Vienna. It has featured in many films, and achieved special fame in "The Third Man".

VIENNA AND WINE

Vienna is said to be the only city in the world with a wine-growing industry within its boundaries. With almost 700 hectares of vineyards Vienna is one of the four largest wine producing areas in Austria.

The mediaeval Emperor Karl der Grosse (Charles the Great or Charlemagne) promoted wine cultivation around Vienna, and by the 14th century the town had become the centre of wine production in the Danube region.

By 1456, however, these wines had become unpalatable, so that Emperor Friedrich III is reputed to have

ordered the use of wine to mix the mortar for the building of St. Stephen's Cathedral.

Maria Theresia and her son Joseph II both encouraged the wine culture, which experienced a fresh stimulus under their rule.

In 1784 Emperor Joseph II decreed that all growers could sell their home-produced wines all year round, and thereby established the institution of today's Heurigen taverns.

This unique form of tavern is still highly popular among Viennese and tourists alike, who all enjoy the convivial atmosphere of the vintner houses and "Buschenschanken" around the outskirts of the city.

The linguistic roots of the Heurigen go back to mediaeval times. In Middle High German the current year's wine pressing was known as "hiu jaru". In modern German "heuer" means "this year", and the mediaeval expression has developed into the modern "Heurigen".

MODERN VIENNA

1. The Crown Prince Rudolf Bridge, opened in 1876, was the first crossing of the Danube main stream after its regulation. The suspension bridge that replaced it in 1937 collapsed in 1976, and was replaced with the present Reichsbrücke. United Nations HQ Vienna is in the background.

2. Headquarters of the OMV international oil concern

3. The Skyline of the Copa Cagrana pleasure strand on the Danube Island. At the end of June every year this is the scene of Europe's largest open-air festival.

4. The Haas Haus on the Stephansplatz, by architect Hans Hollein, 1990 (I5)

5. The 7,000 m² facade of the Uniqa Tower has an LED surface to give various light effects. Designer was Heinz Neumann, 2004 (M3)

6. It is not just the sound of the waltz that is heard in Vienna. There is no lack of opportunities for fans of electronic music. The Flex (I1) and the Praterdome (Q1) are two of the most popular discotheques in the city.

HUNDERTWASSER-KRAWINAHOUSE

1030 Vienna,
Kegelgasse 34-38 (Q6)

Co-authors of the original: Arch.Univ.-Prof. Josef Krawina jointly with Friedensreich Hundertwasser (1979 -1985)

Professor Joseph Krawina, the architect, intended this house to be a pilot project for future ecological social housing.

The Hundertwasser-KrawinaHouse is one of the most-visited buildings in Austria, and in this sense belongs to the country's most important cultural objects. It is a colourful, fairy-tale castle bedecked with greenery, amidst the greyness of the surrounding city buildings. It is a house that meets the desire for harmony, individuality and civilized values.

During the late 1970s the prominent Austrian painter Friedensreich Hundertwasser presented a proposal to the City Council that it should build a house based on ecological principles, and that it should entrust him with its design. His basic idea was to have plenty of greenery, and in particular that the roof should be planted with trees. In 1979, exactly 60 years after the building of the first social housing by the

city, the Vienna city administration commissioned the architect Joseph Krawina, who was known for his ecological building standards, to cooperate with Hundertwasser in drafting an appropriate design. The ecological house was to create a nature-conscious living space that would offer a contrast to the architecture of post-war Vienna. The Hundertwasser-KrawinaHouse laid the foundation for succeeding artistic building projects by Hundertwasser.

Overall, Hundertwasser completed around 50 architectural and façade design projects, of which more than half were realised worldwide. None of these succeeding projects, however, has come anywhere near the success of the ground-breaking Vienna idea in terms of visitor numbers and publications. The reason for this unprecedented success may well be sought in the fruitful blending of the genius of the established and experienced architect with that of the emotionally and imaginatively gifted artist.

It can be readily assumed that, with this initial project as well as his later – and sometimes controversial – collaboration with Krawina, Hundertwasser was able to amass the experience that he invested in his later building work in a number of other countries around the world.

VIENNA THROUGH THE AGES

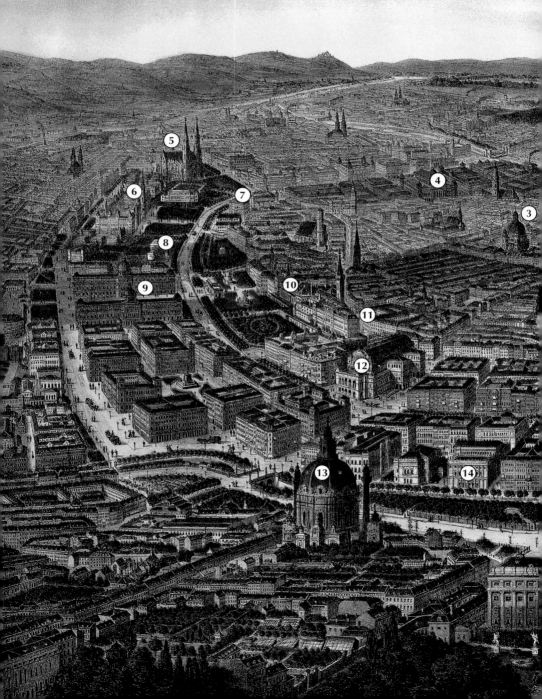

Chromolithography by Würbel after G. Veith, "Panorama of Vienna", 1873

1. St. Stephen's
2. Jesuit Church
3. St. Peter's
4. Old Stock Exchange
5. Votive Church
6. City Hall
7. Burgtheater
8. Parliament
9. Art/Science Museums
10. Old Hofburg
11. Albertina
12. State Opera
13. St. Charles Borromeo
14. Musikverein
15. Schwarzenberg Palace
16. Lower Belvedere

The story of the former Habsburg capital city of Vienna, which for most of its brilliant history was the centre of the Holy Roman Empire of the German Nation, begins at the time of the Roman Empire.

Up to the year 488 AD there was a Roman legionary camp and a small civilian settlement called **Vindobona** where Vienna now stands.

The collapse of the West Roman Empire, and the withdrawal of the Roman soldiers from the Danube region at the end of the 5th century AD, put an end to the camp and the civilian town. The next evidence of settlement in the Danube valley dates from the early 9th century. Under the three German emperors named Otto, what was called "Wenia" belonged to the Bavarian Ostmark (eastern land). The town was soon firmly anchored in the Holy Roman Empire, and by the 12th century it was one of the most important trading centres in Central Europe.

As the second-largest town in the Empire, after Köln (Cologne), Vienna was awarded city status in the year 1221.

In 1251 the Bohemian king **Ottokar II Přemysl** brought the city under his

Maximilian I

rule, when he completed the fortification of the citadel that had been started under the Babenberg ducal dynasty.

In 1276, however, he lost out to **Rudolf von Habsburg**, and as a result had to give up Vienna to him. The Habsburgs ruled Austria for the next 640 years.

Despite some initial unrest, the Habsburgs succeeded in developing Vi-

Leopold I

enna into one of the most splendid cities of the Empire by the time of **Rudolf IV**, who founded the University.

In the 15th century, **Friedrich III** became the first Habsburg to ascend the throne of the Holy Roman Empire of the German Nation. From this point on, the crown of the Holy Roman Empire remained in Habsburg hands with only brief interruptions.

The marriage of **Maximilian I** to the heiress Maria von Burgund represented another enhancement of Habsburg power. Their grandson **Karl V** was soon the most powerful ruler in Europe. Nonetheless, Karl had to abdicate voluntarily, because the Reformation was threatening the peace of the Empire. Astonishingly, the crown remained in Habsburg hands. This demonstrated once again the power that this family exercised over all classes in the population, and over the state itself. They awarded themselves the titles of **Archduke** and **Archduchess**, a degree higher than Duke and Duchess, and a rank that had never previously existed.

Nevertheless, the power of the Habsburg dynasty was repeatedly put to the test during the following centuries.

In 1529 a Turkish army besieged Vienna for the first time, and the Habsburgs were also deeply involved in the Thirty Years' War. When that war ended in 1648 with the Peace of Westphalia, the Empire was reorganised in a loose federation of innumerable small principalities that had to be held together somehow.

In July 1683 the Turks besieged Vienna for the second time, but made the mistake of failing to secure their rear. And so the relieving coalition army under King Jan Sobieski of Poland descended on them from the heights of the Kahlenberg, and in two hours Vienna was free.

It was **Emperor Leopold I** who brought the crown of Hungary to the Habsburgs. His eldest son **Joseph** was crowned King of Hungary in 1687, and in 1690 almost unanimously as German King.

Under **Emperor Ferdinand I** (1503-1564) Vienna became the capital of the Habsburg Monarchy. For centuries the town consisted only of what is now the Inner City, but in 1698 it expanded to incorporate its immediate suburbs.

The settlement pattern

Joseph I

of the population changed along with the expansion. The aristocrats, desirous of residing near to the imperial court, often bought several adjoining middle-class town houses in order to erect imposing palaces on their sites, and the lower classes were increasingly forced to move outwards to the suburbs.

In 1679 and 1713 two major epidemics of bubonic plague raged through

Karl VI

the city. Despite these, around 1700 Vienna experienced the full flowering of its status as one of the most important trading cities in Europe. Economic success, and the end of the Turkish threat, led to the flowering of baroque architecture, and to some of Vienna's most magnificent buildings.

Emperor Karl VI, who ascended the throne in 1711, was plagued by the fear that he would die without a male heir. He therefore compiled the **Pragmatic Sanction**, which united all the lands of the Empire, and appointed his daughter **Maria Theresia** to be his successor.

Karl knew that the Sanction would be controversial and difficult to implement, and so he kept it secret for seven years, until the death of his only son removed the last chance of a Habsburg male heir.

Franz I Stephan von Lothringen (Lorraine) abandoned his dynastic claims during the War of the Polish Succession in order to marry Austrian heiress Maria Theresia and become the next Emperor.

From then to the present day, the dynasty has been titled **Habsburg-Lothringen**.

After Karl's death the War of the Austrian Succession broke out, because a number of the ruling houses of Europe refused to recognise the Pragmatic Sanction. However, Maria Theresia was able to assert her claim to the Austrian throne.

The Archduchess and Empress turned her Austrian inheritance into a bureaucratic state, with the military as its most important element. The power of the Catholic Church was increasingly restricted, and a compulsory state school system was introduced for all children.

Her son and successor **Josef II** was elected Emperor in 1764.

The "Josephine" era brought further measures towards developing the Monarchy into a bureaucratic state.

Josef's policy of reforming the Empire and extending his own power was to fail on the opposition of **Friedrich der Grosse** (Frederick the Great, King of Prussia).

In 1784 Josef decreed that the official language of the state would henceforth be German, instead of Latin, and thereby attracted the hostility of the Hungarians. Josef, whose only aim was to consoli-

Franz I Stephan von Lothringen

date the Empire, finally achieved the exact opposite. When he died in February 1790, he left his brother **Leopold II** a disrupted state.

Emperor Leopold II succeeded in pacifying the Hungarians, but this was overshadowed by another danger, because the revolutionary wind blowing from France was threatening to engulf the whole of

Maria Theresia

Europe. His death in 1792 ended the reform era of enlightened absolutism. Since the excesses of the French Revolution the Enlightenment idea had long since lost its attraction by the time the "Good Franz", the last Emperor of the Holy Roman Empire of the German Nation, ascended the throne.

In 1795 and 1802 **Emperor Franz II** had forbidden the establishment of factories in the Inner City and suburbs of Vienna, whereby industry became concentrated far outside on the city periphery, to the detriment of the inner districts.

During the Napoleonic era the French army twice occupied Vienna, in 1805 and 1809. On both occasions **Napoleon** himself stayed in Schönbrunn Palace.

The second occupation led to the "Peace of Schönbrunn", that was intended to reduce Austria to a second-rank state. And in fact, in 1811, Austria had to declare itself bankrupt.

On 14 August 1804, in Vienna, Franz proclaimed the inauguration of the **Austrian Empire**, since he already anticipated that the mighty Holy Roman Empire was on the point of collapse. And he was right. In 1806, under pressure by Napoleon, 16 member states combined to form the **Rheinische Bundesstaaten** (Rhineland Confederation), and proclaimed that they no longer belonged to the Empire.

The Emperor's answer came by return: Franz II abdicated the imperial crown and proclaimed the Holy Roman Empire of the German Nation (founded by Charlemagne in 800 AD) to be at an end. From that point on he would be **Franz I, Emperor of Austria**.

The Allied victory over Napoleon in 1814 led to the **Congress of Vienna** to redraw the map of Europe. In 1816 the Austrian National Bank was founded, and with the stabilisation of the currency the situation in the Monarchy became more settled.

In 1817 the Emperor was able to declare the fortress status of his capital city to be at an end.

His son and heir **Emperor Ferdinand I** had a number of talents, but government was not one of them.

In 1848 revolution broke out in Vienna. The participating masses soon divided into those who had ideological and social objectives, and those who

Emperor Franz Joseph I

were simply out for more money and a higher standard of living.

This lack of unanimity, combined with the military action that was taken to suppress the uprising, was the main reason for its ultimate failure.

When **Prince Felix von Schwarzenberg** was called upon to form a new Cabinet, the first thing he did was to demand the abdica-

Empress Elisabeth

tion of the Emperor in favour of his young nephew, Archduke Franz Joseph. He received solid support in this from Franz Joseph's mother, **Archduchess Sophie**.

And so the 55-year-old Emperor Ferdinand left the stage and was succeeded by the 18-year-old **Emperor Franz Joseph I** as head of the Austrian Monarchy.

The Hungarians, however, declined to recognise the young Emperor, and demanded their own sovereign Hungarian state. When they proclaimed themselves a republic in 1849, the rebellion could be suppressed only with Russian military assistance.

After the crushing of the revolutionaries, the spectre of a possible further rebellion haunted Vienna. A ring of military barracks was built to maintain security around the Inner City.

Franz Joseph took the reins of government firmly into his hand, and transformed the Monarchy into an absolutist state. The army once more became the main prop of the Monarchy, and the Emperor from time to time took over the supreme command in person.

He concentrated as much power as possible in

*Vienna 1683. The city's defensive walls can be seen.
In the mid-19th century the Ringstrasse was built on their site.*

the outer suburbs, giving the city more or less its present dimensions.

In 1853 there was an unsuccessful attempt on the life of the young Emperor Franz Joseph. The Votivkirche, built just outside Vienna's defensive wall to commemorate his survival, was to have a strong influence on the city's urban development. It was then that the idea arose of demolishing the military fortifications and replacing them with a major ring road that would have a military as well as a civilian character.

In 1854 Franz Joseph married **Elisabeth** of Bavaria, who in 1858 gave birth to **Crown**

his own person. He personally presided over the Cabinet, and took all the important political decisions himself.

In 1850 Vienna expanded again to assimilate

"Pipe smoking, the wealth of the people is squandered!" In 1890 it was not just enthusiasm that greeted the Ringstrasse architecture. Today, it still endows Vienna with the splendour of a metropolis.

Prince Rudolf, the heir to the Austrian throne.

In the same year, 1858, the Emperor gave the order to demolish the Vienna city walls.

This politically and historically significant event opened the way for the building of the Ringstrasse, the majestic boulevard surrounding the Inner City that gives Vienna so much of its unique character (pages 42-43).

In 1867 Franz Joseph and Elisabeth were crowned King and Queen of Hungary after a reconciliation with the Hungarians. A constitutional agreement that year set up the Dual Monarchy of Austria-Hungary, which Franz Joseph ruled as Emperor of Austria and King of Hungary.

Despite the 1873 stock exchange crash the Viennese economy was able to show an upswing, not least due to the World Exhibition that was held there that year.

By the end of the 19th century the most important historic buildings on the Ringstrasse had all been completed.

The developments also indicated a political move in the direction of greater democracy.

On the other hand, there was considerable public criticism of the ostentatious private buildings along the Ringstrasse. The aristocracy flaunted its wealth while the people were confronted with ever higher rents.

Emperor Franz Joseph suffered several hard blows during this period.

The Imperial and Royal Court Opera, opened on 25 May 1869, was "the first house on the "Ring" (H7)

3

4

The fact that Vienna is on UNESCO's World Heritage List is primarily due to the great interest shown by the Habsburgs in art, culture, music, and the representative impression created by their capital city.

1. *View from the historic Elisabeth Bridge to the Church of St. Charles Borromeo*

2. *The new University building, opened in 1884, was a further prestigious addition to the Ringstrasse (E3)*

3. *The Harrach and Ferstel palaces on the Freyung square (F4)*

4. *St. Stephen's Cathedral (I5)*

Ofen den 16. April 1868.

Lieber Rudolph,

Morgen ist dein Namenstag und
ich kann denselben leider nicht mit
dir zubringen und nur in Gedanken
mich zu dir und Gisela näher machen.
Von ganzem Herzen wünsche ich dir
alles Gute, Gott erhalte und beschütze
dich und geb es in Seiner Gnade,
daß wir nur immer Freude und
Trost an dir erleben, wie es bis
jetzt immer der Fall war. Sei
nur recht gehorsam, fleißig und
gewissenhaft in Lernen. Thue nur was
recht ist, so wirst du ein braver
tüchtiger Mann werden.

Ich hoffe, daß unser Geschenk dir

Crown Prince Rudolf

The death of the heir to the thrones of Austria-Hungary entered the history books as the **Mayerling Affair**, which brought **Archduke Franz Ferdinand** to the fore as the new Crown Prince.

In 1898 an anarchist assassinated **Empress Elisabeth** during a visit to Geneva. Stabbed with a hand

Baroness Mary Vetsera

In 1889 Crown Prince Rudolf committed suicide with his mistress, the 17-year-old Baroness Mary Vetsera, in his hunting lodge in Mayerling.

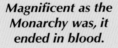

Magnificent as the Monarchy was, it ended in blood.

file, she succumbed to her injury a few hours later.

Then, on 28 June 1914, Franz Ferdinand and his wife were murdered by a revolutionary in Sarajevo, capital of Bosnia, an event that ultimately led to the outbreak of the First World War. Franz Joseph died in November 1916, during the war, after a reign of 68 years.

The last official document signed by his successor, **Emperor Karl I**, in November 1918 after the end of the war, was his withdrawal from the affairs of state. He specifically did not abdicate the imperial crown. His wife, **Empress Zita**, right until her death in 1989, insisted on her titles as Empress of Austria and Queen of Hungary.

The attack on Empress Elisabeth in Geneva on 10 September 1898

1. *Emperor Franz Joseph's letter to his son, Crown Prince Rudolf, dated 16 April 1868*

The Author

Lina Schnorr was born in Worms on 12 February 1986. Educated at the Freie Waldorfschule Frankenthal, after leaving school she moved to Austria to study Sinology at the University of Vienna. Since 2006 she has also worked for the information service at the Hundertwasser-KrawinaHouse. This activity led her to a more detailed study of the history of Vienna, and finally provided the inspiration for the present book.

The Photographer and Publisher

Harald Böhm was born in Linz on 20 February 1965. After graduating from the TGM higher technical school he went on to study business management at the University of Economics in Vienna, afterwards specialising in economic informatics at the Johannes Kepler University in Linz. After graduation he took over the management of his family firm (beauty appeal GesmbH) and founded the H.B. Medienvertrieb GesmbH, which provides the public information service for the Hundertwasser-KrawinaHouse.

This book is affectionately dedicated in gratitude to my mother, Linda Böhm.

Picture and Text Sources

Co-author: Veronika Siegmund
English text: Dr. James Wilkie
Reader: Dr. Helga Zoglmann
Inside cover - genealogical table: Johanna Hess
Inside cover -Vienna city plan: Jana Sagner
p. 21: Hofburg plan: Christina Wendt & Jennifer Vollstuber
pp. 32-33: Spanish Riding School Archive, www.srs.at
p. 69: Robert Hoffmann, www.luftbildaufnahmen.at
p. 74 and p. 75 bottom: Richard Schuster, www.fotoschuster.com
p. 80 below left: Liechtenstein Museum Archive, www.liechtensteinmuseum.at
p.84 centre top: DI Klaus Egger
pp. 88-89: Wolfgang Feil, Freigabenummer 36.379/1966
p. 91 bottom right: Peter M. Böhm, www.pressepic.at
p. 113 bottom right: Wolfgang Oesterreicher
p. 115 left and top right: Gregor Semrad, www.gregorsemrad.com
pp. 116-117: Würbel after Veith "Panorama of Vienna", 1873, Vienna City Museum, www.viennamuseum.at
p. 122: "Ringstrassenbarone" cartoon 18.09.1890, ÖNB, 399.875-D. Neu Per Kikeriki, 1890, No. 75, S.4
p. 126: Franz Joseph letter 1868,ÖStA, HHStA HA Selekt Kronprinz Rudolf K.18.

Bibliography

(Ed.) Bundesdenkmalamt (2003): Dehio Wien. 1. Bezirk – Innere Stadt. Verlag Berger, Horn/Vienna.
(Ed.) Csendes, Peter / Opll, Ferdinand (2006): Wien. Geschichte einer Stadt. Von 1790 bis zur Gegenwart. Böhlau, Vienna.
Dmytrasz, Barbara (2008): Die Ringstrasse. Eine Europäische Bauidee. Verlag Amalthea Signum, Vienna.
Etzlstorfer, Hannes / Hajni, István (2007): Habsburg. Die schönsten Residenzen. Verlag Kremayr & Scheriau/Orac, Vienna.
Herm, Gerhard (1989): Glanz und Niedergang des Hauses Habsburg. Verlag Econ, Düsseldorf.
Iby, Elfriede / Koller, Alexander (2007): Schönbrunn. Verlag Christian Brandstätter, Vienna.
Kraus, Wolfgang / Müller, Peter (1991): Wiener Palais. Verlag Blanckenstein, Munich.

ISBN: 978-3-9502396-9-0
© H.B. Medienvertrieb GesmbH, 3rd edition 2012
Kegelgasse 34-38, A-1030 Vienna
www.imperialvienna.info
Graphics and reproduction: Fotografie Mitterbauer GmbH&CoKG, A-4950 Altheim